TRIANGLE HISTORIES

THE CIVIL WAR

JOHN BROWN

Helaine Becker

BLACKBIRCH PRESS, INC.

WOODBRIDGE, CONNECTICUT

Published by Blackbirch Press, Inc.
260 Amity Road
Woodbridge, CT 06525
Web site: http://www.blackbirch.com
e-mail: staff@blackbirch.com
© 2001 Blackbirch Press, Inc.

Printed in China

10 9 8 7 6 5 4 3 2 1

Photo credits:
Cover, pages 4, 6, 19, 21, 26, 29, 31, 35, 37, 50, 52, 57, 65, 88, 91:
©North Wind Picture Archives; cover (inset), pages 8, 24, 25, 32, 42, 45,
55, 69, 79, 84, 87, 94, 98, 100: The Library of Congress; pages 10, 13, 34,
39, 48: National Archives; pages 15, 60: National Portrait Gallery; pages 72,
74, 76-77, 79, 80-81, 82-83, 90, 92: National Park Service.

Library of Congress Cataloging-in-Publication Data
Becker, Helaine.
John Brown / by Helaine Becker.
        p. cm. — (The Civil War)
Includes index.
Summary: Examines the life of abolitionist John Brown, the people and
events surrounding the raid he led on the arsenal at Harper's Ferry, West
Virginia, in 1859, and its aftermath.
        ISBN 1-56711-558-6 (hardcover : alk. paper)
1. Brown, John, 1800–1859.—Juvenile literature. 2. Abolitionists—United
States—Biography—Juvenile literature. 3. Antislavery movements—United
States—History—19th Century—Juvenile literature. [1. Brown, John,
1800–1859. 2. Abolitionists. 3. Harper's Ferry (W. Va.)—History—John
Brown's Raid, 1859. 4. Antislavery movements.] I. Title. II. Civil War
(Blackbirch Press)

E451 .B43 2001   2001002571
973.7'116—dc21

CONTENTS

Preface: The Civil War   4

Introduction:
"The Wind Blew
His Lifeless Body To and Fro"   8

Chapter 1   Born into a New Century   11

Chapter 2   Westward Expansion and Abolition   27

Chapter 3   "Bleeding Kansas"   43

Chapter 4   The Secret Six   61

Chapter 5   The Raid on Harpers Ferry   73

Chapter 6   Aftermath   95

Glossary   101

For More Information   102

Index   103

PREFACE: THE CIVIL WAR

Nearly 150 years after the final shots were fired, the Civil War remains one of the key events in U. S. history. The enormous loss of life alone makes it tragically unique: More Americans died in Civil War battles than in all other American wars combined. More Americans fell at the Battle of Gettysburg than during any battle in American military history. And, in one day at the Battle of Antietam, more Americans were killed and wounded than in any other day in American history.

Slaves did the backbreaking work on Southern plantations.

As tragic as the loss of life was, however, it is the principles over which the war was fought that make it uniquely American. Those beliefs—equality and freedom—are the foundation of American democracy, our basic rights. It was the bitter disagreement about the exact nature of those rights that drove our nation to its bloodiest war.

The disagreements grew in part from the differing economies of the North and South. The warm climate and wide-open areas of the Southern states were ideal for an economy based on agriculture. In the first half of the 19th century, the main cash crop was cotton, grown on large farms called plantations. Slaves, who were brought to the United States from Africa, were forced to do the backbreaking work of planting and harvesting cotton. They also provided the other labor necessary to keep plantations running. Slaves were bought and sold like property, and had been critical to the Southern economy since the first Africans came to America in 1619.

The suffering of African Americans under slavery is one of the great tragedies in American history. And the debate over whether the United States government had the right to forbid slavery—in both Southern states and in new territories—was a dispute that overshadowed the first 80 years of our history.

For many Northerners, the question of slavery was one of morality and not economics. Because the Northern economy was based on manufacturing rather than agriculture, there was little need for slave labor. The primary economic need of Northern states was a protective tax known as a tariff that would make imported goods more expensive than goods made in the North. Tariffs forced Southerners to buy Northern goods and made them economically dependent on the North, a fact that led to deep resentment among Southerners.

Economic control did not matter to the anti-slavery Northerners known as abolitionists. Their conflict with the South was over slavery. The idea that the federal government could outlaw slavery was perfectly reasonable. After all, abolitionists contended, our nation was founded on the idea that all people are created equal. How could slavery exist in such a country?

For the Southern states that joined the Confederacy, the freedom from unfair taxation and the right to make their

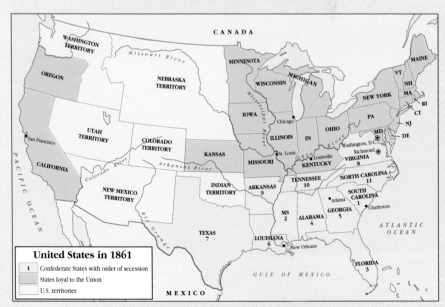

own decisions about slavery was as important a principle as equality. For most Southerners, the right of states to decide what is best for its citizens was the most important principle guaranteed in the Constitution.

The conflict over these principles generated sparks throughout the decades leading up to the Civil War. The importance of keeping an equal number of slave and free states in the Union became critical to Southern lawmakers in Congress in those years. In 1820, when Maine and Missouri sought admission to the Union, the question was settled by the Missouri Compromise: Maine was admitted as a free state, Missouri as a slave state, thus maintaining a balance in Congress. The compromise stated that all future territories north of the southern boundary of Missouri would enter the Union as free states, those south of it would be slave states.

In 1854, however, the Kansas-Nebraska Act set the stage for the Civil War. That act repealed the Missouri Compromise and by declaring that the question of slavery should be decided by residents of the territory, set off a rush of pro- and anti-slavery settlers to the new land. Violence between the two sides began almost immediately and soon "Bleeding Kansas" became a tragic chapter in our nation's story.

With Lincoln's election on an anti-slavery platform in 1860, the disagreement over the power of the federal government reached its breaking point. In early 1861, South Carolina became the first state to secede from the Union, followed by Mississippi, Florida, Alabama, Georgia, Louisiana, Virginia, Texas, North Carolina, Tennessee, and Arkansas. Those eleven states became the Confederate States of America. Confederate troops fired the first shots of the Civil War at Fort Sumter, South Carolina, on April 12, 1861. Those shots began a four-year war in which thousands of Americans—Northerners and Southerners—would give, in President Lincoln's words, "the last full measure of devotion."

OPPOSITE: The Confederate attack on Fort Sumter began the Civil War.

INTRODUCTION:
"THE WIND BLEW HIS LIFELESS BODY TO AND FRO"

Late in the morning of December 2, 1859, a wagon carrying a coffin of black walnut rolled towards a gallows in Harpers Ferry, Virginia. Sitting on top of the coffin was a wiry man with a thick, tangled beard that reached the middle of his chest He wore red slippers, white socks, black pants, a black vest, and a long black coat. The collar of his white linen shirt was open. The man's arms were tied elbow to elbow, close to his sides, leaving his forearms and hands dangling in front of him.

Rows of heavily armed soldiers marched on all sides of the wagon. Around the gallows, rows of cadets from the Virginia Military Institute stood at attention. Like the soldiers, these young men had come to witness the execution of a man who had attempted to start a slave rebellion. They had their guns ready in case his followers attempted to free

John Brown rode on top of his own coffin on the way to his execution in 1859.

him. Among the commanders of the cadets was Major Thomas Jackson. Later, he would be known as "Stonewall" Jackson, the military genius of the Confederacy during the Civil War.

At that moment, however, there was no Confederacy, and no Civil War. If the man in black had succeeded in his plan, many there knew, the slaves of Virginia, and possibly much of the South, would have been in armed revolt.

For now, though, there was only an old man in slippers climbing the scaffold to face the hangman. Oddly, he seemed cheerful, shaking hands with several officials who stood around him. A sheriff placed a rope around his neck and a hood over his face. Asked if he wished a signal when the trap door was ready to be open, the man replied, "It makes no difference, providing I'm not kept waiting too long."

It took ten minutes for the apparatus to be readied. Suddenly, the trap door swung open and the man dropped, his knees reaching the level where his feet had been a split second before. His forearms flew up, hands tight, then gradually fell into spasms of death.

John Brown was dead.

Jackson described the event in a letter to his wife. "John Brown was hung today at about 11:30 A.M. He behaved with unflinching firmness," wrote Jackson. After the trap door fell open, "there was very little motion for several minutes, after which the wind blew his lifeless body to and fro."

9

Chapter 1

BORN INTO
A NEW CENTURY

John Brown was born in Torrington, Connecticut, on May 9, 1800. His family was poor, but respected by townspeople. As a child, Brown was told that one of his father's ancestors had come with the Puritans to America on the *Mayflower*. His mother was descended from an early settler of New England. Members on both sides of the family had fought in the Revolutionary War.

OPPOSITE: John Brown was born and raised in the North and was part of a deeply religious family that believed the Bible forbade slavery.

In 1800, the United States was not quite 25 years old. The practice of slavery in the country, however, was almost 180 years old. In fact, the first African slaves had arrived in Virginia a year before the *Mayflower* landed. Importing slaves from Africa would not become illegal in the new country for another seven years.

In Brown's home state of Connecticut, slaves had worked on farms in cities since the mid-1600s. In the year John Brown was born, nearly 20 percent of the African Americans in the Northern state were slaves. Only three years earlier, Connecticut lawmakers has passed a bill granting freedom to all slaves when they reached the age of twenty-one. Freed slaves could not travel in the state without passes, however, and could not testify against whites in court. Such deep-rooted prejudice would lead the Connecticut legislature to deny black men the right to vote until after the Civil War.

Slavery was more common in the South, though most Southerners—like most Northerners—did not own slaves. In Virginia, the state where slaves were first brought ashore, laws allowed slaves to travel and meet freely on evenings and weekends. Plantation owners hired out skilled slaves who earned a small wage and had the chance to travel beyond their community.

In 1800, freedom was more than a dream for some African Americans in Virginia. Slaves who earned money might actually buy their freedom. Legislators passed laws giving owners the right to

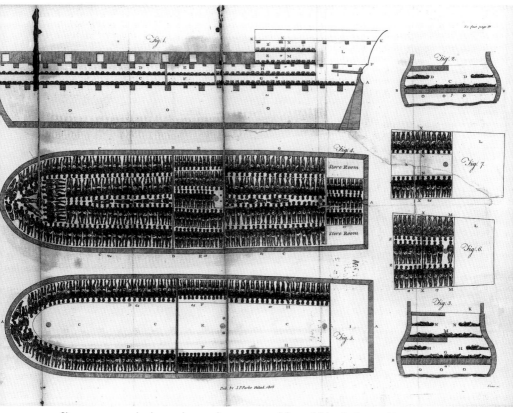

Slaves were packed together and transported from Africa in large ships like this one.

free slaves. Religious groups had formed abolition societies across Virginia. Over 10 percent of Richmond's African-American population was free.

Those dreams changed in the summer of 1800. In July, a slave named Gabriel Prosser gathered slaves from other plantations in southern Virginia to plan a widespread rebellion that would destroy slavery in Virginia. The slaves planned to kill plantation owners and capture the state capital in Richmond. They would then kidnap Governor

13

James Monroe—who would later become the fifth president of the United States—and persuade him to accept their demands.

The plan was set for August 30, 1800. It failed, however, when thunderstorms washed out roads and bridges in the area. The attack was set for the next evening, but it was too late. Two slaves told their owner of the plot. The owner notified Governor Monroe, who called out the militia to protect the Capital.

On September 23, 1800, Prosser was arrested and imprisoned. He was executed at the gallows on October 10, 1800, the last of twenty-six rebellious slaves to die. As a result of the failure of "Gabriel's Revolt," lawmakers restricted slave travel and communication. Abolition societies closed operations in Virginia. Free blacks had to leave the state within six months.

Up North, John Brown, who would grow up to be slavery's violent enemy, was not yet a year old. His lifetime struggle still lay ahead of him. Brown's parents were devout Calvinists, a very strict Protestant denomination that believed every word of the Bible was absolutely true. Bible reading was part of daily home life. Young John was trained to "fear God and keep his commandments." He claimed to have memorized most of the Bible by the time he was a young man. The Browns, like many other deeply religious people, believed that the Bible forbade slavery, and John grew up believing that slavery was a sin.

James Monroe was targeted for kidnapping in an attempted slave rebellion that was planned for August 1800.

John's father died when his little boy was only five. A few years later, his mother remarried. Young John moved with his mother and stepfather to Ohio, to an area already known for its anti-slavery attitudes. At that time, Ohio was the western frontier of the young United States. There were no public schools, so John spent most of his time outdoors. He learned many pioneer skills, from handling guns to dressing deerskins and making his own leather.

John grew up strong and large for his age. He was, in his own words, "excessively fond of the hardest and roughest kind of play." He had no interest in education or school. He did have access to a good library, however, and reading on his own helped him avoid trouble. What education he did receive, Brown later claimed, came from reading history and biographies at the library.

John's mother died when he was eight years old. His stepfather soon remarried and, though John liked his stepmother, he never got over the loss of his mother. He spoke sadly of her death for most of his life.

★

Abraham Lincoln and Stonewall Jackson also lost their mothers at a young age.

★

When he was twelve, a key event took place in John's life, which further hardened his views about slavery. Being a mature and responsible young person for his age, John was given the job of bringing a herd of cattle to its new owner in the wilderness of Michigan. Along the way, he stayed for a time in the home of a slave owner. One slave there was a young boy of about the same age as John. He found the boy to be warm and intelligent, and the two became friends almost right away.

During his stay, Brown was well treated by his host and praised for his ability to herd cattle over such a distance. He ate at the host's dinner table as an honored guest. At the same time, John's heart sunk as he saw the slave boy being badly mistreated. Many years later, Brown wrote of the event in a letter. "The Negro boy who was fully if not more than my equal, was badly clothed, poorly fed and lodged in cold weather; and beaten before my eyes with Iron Shovels or any other thing that first came to hand."

"Like a King"

John Brown grew into stubborn and arrogant man through his teens. His younger brother often teased him, saying he was, "like a King against whom there is no rising up."

Brown actually agreed with his brother's words. He described himself as "having tenacity" and claimed that he "rarely failed" in tasks he took on. He expected to succeed at everything he did, so he became "conceited" and "self-confident." As someone who had assumed adult responsibilities at an early age, he also expected to be obeyed. Along with this expectation, he developed the habit of speaking down to people. Those closest to Brown said that he had no sense of humor, no hobbies, and no interests beside his work.

In 1817, at about the time the "self-confident" John Brown was entering adulthood in Ohio, a child was born to a slave woman on a farm in eastern Maryland, a few hundred miles away. The child, Frederick Bailey, never knew his father, who was a white man. Like Brown, however, he lost his mother at an early age. Like Brown, he would teach himself to read and write. And, like Brown, he would speak out forcefully against slavery. When he did, he would be known as Frederick Douglass. And he would suffer countless whippings and other brutalities before he crossed paths with the fiery John Brown.

Back in Ohio, Brown considered becoming a minister, but he found the intense study of religion too difficult because of his poor education. He gave up this idea and joined his stepfather in the family tanning business, making cowhide into leather. Brown had worked for his stepfather while growing up, and knew the business well, but the young man was stubborn and simply would not take orders. Independent minded, Brown soon left home and opened a tannery of his own that competed with his stepfather's.

Brown's new business was successful. By 1820, he had earned enough money to marry Dianthe Lusk, whom he later described as "a remarkably plain, but neat, industrious and economical girl; of excellent character; earnest piety; and good practical, common sense."

In that same year, the debate over slavery reached the halls of Congress for the first time. A year earlier, the territory of Missouri asked to be admitted to the Union. Since slavery was permitted in Missouri Territory, however, the Northern abolitionists had no intention of letting it remain so. They called on their representatives, to deny

John Brown and his stepfather both worked in tanneries, which looked similar to the one above.

John Brown

Missouri's statehood. When Missouri's statehood bill was brought before the U.S. House of Representatives, New York Congressman James Talmadge proposed an amendment restricting slavery within its borders.

The South was shocked by the proposed amendment. They had been blind to the opposition brewing in Congress against new slave states. Other slave states had been admitted to the Union—Alabama had been admitted as a slave state only months earlier with no objection. But Southern legislators overlooked the fact that Alabama's admission meant there were eleven free states and eleven slave states. Admitting Missouri as either free or slave would shift the delicate balance in Congress.

The debates in Congress over the issue revealed for the first time how divided the two regions of the nation had become. The North, for example, saw no injustice in the proposed amendment restricting slavery. Southern lawmakers, however, saw Missouri as "one of their own" —an agricultural region populated by Southerners and their slaves. To them, the Talmadge amendment was a threat to their way of life. Mass meetings were held in towns across America to discuss the proposals. Northern meetings denounced the extension of slavery. Southerners invoked the Constitution, saying that it guaranteed the right to own slaves. Five Northern states passed resolutions protesting Missouri's admission as a slave state.

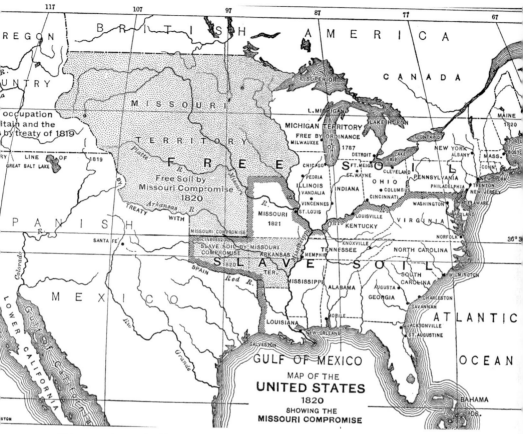

This map shows the United States at the time of the Missouri Compromise. "Free soil" and "slave soil" territories are labled.

Meanwhile, Southern representatives argued that people had the right to determine for themselves what their institutions should be. They insisted that all new states coming into the union should have the same rights as the original thirteen states to choose or reject slavery.

The deadlock was ended with what came to be known as the Missouri Compromise, but which depended largely on another new state, Maine. In early 1820, the House passed a bill to award Maine statehood. When the bill was sent to the Senate, the Missouri petition for statehood was attached to it. Admitting Maine a free state, and Missouri, a slave state, preserved the balance of power between free and slave states. For the moment the problem was solved, but how this balanced approach would work in the future was unsettled. Congress embarked on a new course to find a middle road.

After many weeks of debate, Congress passed the so-called "Missouri Compromise." Under the compromise, slavery would be allowed in Missouri but prohibited in any future states north of the line formed by Missouri's southern border.

★

In 1826, Robert E. Lee entered the U.S. Military Academy at West Point.

★

The Missouri Compromise was a turning point in American history. It was the most important single issue Congress had been forced to deal with until that time. It also marked the final forty years of debate over slavery, something that had been part of the American way of life for 200 years up to that point.

Back in Ohio, the tannery was not proving to be a sufficient enough challenge for the ambitious young Brown. In 1826, he moved his family east to the wilderness of Pennsylvania, where he worked as a postmaster for several years. He and Dianthe also opened another tannery. It was much larger than the first, employing fifteen people. By 1831, Brown was considered a leading citizen in his community.

News did not travel as quickly then as it does today. In the late summer of 1831, however, news of a slave revolt—again in Virginia—traveled far and wide. On August 21, a slave named Nat Turner and six other slaves met to make plans for a violent revolt. Like Brown, Turner had been born in 1800, in the same region of Virginia as Gabriel Prosser, only a week before Prosser was hanged.

At 2:00 A.M., Turner and his men entered the home of his master, where they killed the entire family as they slept. They continued on, killing any white people they came upon. Turner's force soon grew to more than forty slaves, most on horseback. By mid-day on August 22, word of the rebellion had reached whites who formed an armed militia. Soon, Turner's force scattered.

In the end, the slaves had stabbed, shot, and clubbed sixty white people to death. After hiding for several weeks, Turner was finally captured on October 30. He was hanged, and then skinned, on November 11. In all, Virginia executed fifty-five people for the revolt. In the panic that resulted from the event, close to 200 African Americans, including many who had nothing to do with the rebellion, were murdered by white mobs. The state legislature of Virginia considered abolishing slavery, but in a close vote decided to retain the practice and to support the strictest policies toward all African Americans.

Back in Pennsylvania, tragedy of a different kind entered the Brown household. Dianthe died shortly

This engraving depicts the discovery of Nat Turner, who led a slave revolt in Virginia in 1831.

after giving birth to Brown's seventh child in 1832. The newborn also died. Events such as those, tragic as they were, were not unusual in those days. In the early 1800s, doctors did not yet know about bacteria or bacterial disease, nor did they understand the importance of washing their hands or using sterilized instruments.

With Dianthe gone, Brown now faced the difficulty of caring for his five surviving children: John Jr., Jason, Owen, Ruth, and Frederick. The following year, Brown married sixteen-year-old Mary Day. She looked after Brown's children, who loved her in return, and soon had her own. Eventually, John and Mary would have thirteen more children together.

Mary Day married John Brown at the age of sixteen.

By 1835, the Brown family had sunk into full-scale poverty. Desperate to find ways to feed his growing family, Brown began borrowing money, and looking about for opportunities to make cash quickly. Unfortunately, the many opportunities that he pursued only made his financial situation grow even worse.

25

Chapter 2

WESTWARD EXPANSION AND ABOLITION

The 1830s were a time of growth for the United States. For the first half of that decade, the president was Andrew Jackson of Tennessee. "Old Hickory," as he was known, was the first president from the frontier, and the first who had not come from a wealthy background. Jackson firmly believed in the right of Americans to expand across the Appalachian Mountains, west to the Mississippi River, and on across the continent to settle wherever they pleased. There was, however, one complication. Native Americans lived on the best land between the Appalachian Mountains and the Mississippi River.

OPPOSITE: Andrew Jackson was president of the United States during a time of great westward expansion.

27

To Jackson—and many citizens who supported him—Native Americans were simply "savages" who belonged far from "civilized" people. Throughout his term in office, Jackson used every means possible—legal and illegal—to remove Native Americans from their native lands. More than a dozen tribes—among them the Cherokee, Miami, Pottowatomie, and Shawnee—were relocated from their traditional lands in the Midwest and South to the plains of what are today Oklahoma, Kansas, and Nebraska.

The policy of Indian Removal opened enormous areas of land for white settlers. As a result, certain ambitious people began to make huge fortunes in land speculation. These specu- lators were often people who worked for wealthy clients and located land on the frontier for them to buy. For their services they were paid a fee, which they in turn used to buy land of their own. They then sold the land they had bought for a huge profit. It was not unusual for land speculators in the early 1830s to make $1,000 a week—$10,000 in today's dollars.

★

In the 1830s, the average yearly salary for a worker was $250.

★

Some of the best land for wealthy investors and speculators was located in states of the South such as Georgia, Alabama, and Mississippi. The dark soil and hot climate were ideal for growing cotton, and wealthy Southerners began to move inland from the Atlantic coast to build large plantations in the new land.

CONSTITUTION

OF THE

CHEROKEE NATION,

MADE AND ESTABLISHED

AT A

GENERAL CONVENTION OF DELEGATES,

DULY AUTHORISED FOR THAT PURPOSE.

AT

NEW ECHOTA,

JULY 26, 1827.

PRINTED FOR THE CHEROKEE NATION,
AT THE OFFICE OF THE STATESMAN AND PATRIOT,
GEORGIA.

THE CASE

OF

THE CHEROKEE NATION

against

THE STATE OF GEORGIA:

ARGUED AND DETERMINED AT

THE SUPREME COURT OF THE UNITED STATES,

JANUARY TERM 1831.

WITH

AN APPENDIX,

Containing the Opinion of Chancellor Kent on the Case; the Treaties between
the United States and the Cherokee Indians; the Act of Congress of
1802, entitled 'An Act to regulate intercourse with the Indian
tribes, &c.'; and the Laws of Georgia relative to the
country occupied by the Cherokee Indians,
within the boundary of that State.

BY RICHARD PETERS,
COUNSELLOR AT LAW.

Philadelphia:
JOHN GRIGG, 9 NORTH FOURTH STREET.
1831.

President Jackson's Indian Removal Policy disregarded previous agreements and treaties between the U.S. government and Native Americans. Above left: A document from 1827 officially declared a Cherokee nation. Above right: By 1831, the Cherokee brought suit against the U.S. government in an effort to reclaim their land.

Where wealthy Southerners went, slaves went too. In 1830, there were about 2 million slaves in the South, worth about $1 billion. Huge numbers of these slaves were taken to the blistering heat and brutal conditions of the Deep South. Between 1830 and 1840, for example, the slave population of Mississippi grew by 200 percent.

Jackson's Indian Removal Policy also made land available in free states and territories in northern regions. That land, however, was better suited to

29

raising different crops or for small manufacturing companies. Roads in those days, however, were narrow, bumpy trails, unsuited for transporting goods from Indiana and Ohio to Eastern markets.

During the 1820s and 1830s, there was a race to develop quick and efficient means of transportation. The steam locomotive had just been invented, but rail lines had not been laid west of the Appalachians. During those years, most goods traveled by water—along the Atlantic Coast, across the Great Lakes, or along large rivers such as the Ohio, the Mississippi, or the Hudson.

Then, in 1825, the Erie Canal was opened. This human-made waterway ran more than 350 miles across New York State from Lake Erie to the Hudson River, which flowed down to New York City. Suddenly, farmers and small manufacturers were able to send crops and goods all the way from Ohio to one of the largest ports on the East Coast.

A system of canals across America seemed the surest way to move raw materials and finished goods. The Erie Canal was followed by the Morris Canal across New Jersey, connecting Pennsylvania and New York City. The Chesapeake and Ohio Canal connected eastern Ohio with markets in the Middle Atlantic States.

Soon, a "canal boom" began in western Ohio and Indiana. Land speculating drew thousands more people who hoped to make a fortune buying land and selling it to canal-building companies.

The Erie Canal in New York was opened in 1825, during the "canal boom" of the 1820s and 1830s. Canals offered quick and efficient new transportation routes.

John Brown

One of the many drawn in by the canal boom was John Brown. He learned a canal was planned for western Ohio by the Pennsylvania Canal Company and decided to purchase land. It looked like a sure bet; the first canal built in eastern Ohio had sent land prices through the roof. Land bought for as little as $11 an acre was sold at $700 an acre.

Brown believed prices would rise even higher when the next canal came through, linking Indiana and all of Ohio with eastern markets. He convinced friends and relatives to invest with him. He moved his family to Franklin Mills, Ohio, borrowed money, and bought land.

Martin Van Buren took office in 1837, just as economic panic set in.

The Panic of 1837

Brown's dream, however, and the dreams of thousands of other speculators, were shattered in 1837. The economic policies of Andrew Jackson in the early 1830s had badly weakened the U.S. economy. Martin Van Buren took office in 1837, just as the first great depression in American history struck the nation's economy. Banks closed, thousands of people went bankrupt, and businesses collapsed.

The Pennsylvania Canal Company stopped its plans to build its canal through Ohio.

Brown's land was suddenly worthless. Advised by his friends and relatives to sell, he stubbornly refused, holding out the hope that the economy would recover. Brown said he trusted in God to look after his affairs.

But the economy only grew worse. Newspapers mocked the president, calling him "Martin Van Ruin." Brown, like thousands of other Americans, could not pay his debts. In desperation, he tried other schemes, each more reckless and risky than the one before.

He tried breeding sheep, and failed. He opened another tannery, and failed. He tried trading cattle, and failed. Perhaps his most ill-advised venture was an attempt to collect tons of American wool from sheep farmers and travel with it to Britain. The plan was a disaster. The wool that arrived in Britain was filthy and low quality. Britain had more than enough clean, high quality wool raised locally in the country. Without a decent pool of buyers, Brown was forced to sell his wool for much less than it cost the farmers to raise it.

★

In 1842, Abraham Lincoln married Mary Todd Edwards in Springfield, Illinois

★

Brown's plan lost $40,000—a fortune at that time. In 1842, he was forced to declare bankruptcy. Sued by the sheep farmers for their losses, Brown lost virtually everything he owned. He was left with a huge family, a few possessions, and a ruined reputation as a businessman.

33

Abolitionism Spreads

During all his years of hard work, toil, and economic trouble, Brown had never given up his early conviction that slavery was a sin. And throughout the 1830s, growing numbers of Americans like Brown began to raise their voices against slavery. One of the anti-slavery movement's most outspoken leaders was William Lloyd Garrison, a self-educated journalist who began publishing an anti-slavery newspaper, *The Liberator*, in 1831.

At that time, those who spoke against slavery usually appealed to slaveholders to gradually end the practice of slavery. Garrison used the strongest language possible to call for the end of slavery "immediately," and blistered those who did not agree with him, calling them "traitors" and "hypocrites." In 1833, he was one of the first founders of the American Anti-Slavery Society. *The Liberator* and Garrison often aroused violent public reactions. South Carolina passed a law stating that anyone caught handing out copies of *The Liberator* could be fined $5,000 and put in jail.

William Lloyd Garrison was an outspoken abolitionist.

THE LIBERATOR.

OL. I.]   WILLIAM LLOYD GARRISON AND ISAAC KNAPP, PUBLISHERS.   [NO. 22.

BOSTON, MASSACHUSETTS.]   OUR COUNTRY IS THE WORLD—OUR COUNTRYMEN ARE MANKIND.   [SATURDAY, MAY 28, 1831.

The Liberator was William Lloyd Garrison's anti-slavery newspaper.

In 1835, a pro-slavery mob dragged Garrison through the streets of Boston by a rope. The mayor of Boston put Garrison in jail and charged him with disturbing the peace for the incident.

Brown, too, was becoming an even more violent opponent of slavery. At the funeral of an abolitionist publisher who had been shot to death by a pro-slavery mob, Brown got to his feet and made a fiery speech, swearing that he would fight to end slavery, no matter what the cost.

Even after his bankruptcy, Brown supported anti-slavery causes. He contributed money to fund abolitionist publications and speeches. He and his wife, Mary, took in a black child and raised him as their own son. Brown insisted that his churches, which were normally segregated at that time, admit blacks as full members. He gave away land to fugitive slaves, and offered his home as a station on the Underground Railroad—a system of homes and other hiding places used by abolitionists to help slaves escape to freedom in Canada.

35

Slave Narratives

★ ★ ★ ★ ★

During the late 1700s, a new type of literature appeared in the United States. The authors were slaves who had been freed or who had escaped and wrote under an assumed name. The books were known as slave narratives. The stories told of the hardship and brutality of life as a slave. Most narratives ended with the stirring adventure of an escape to freedom.

Slave narratives became tremendously popular in 1830s and 1840s, as the abolitionist movement gained strength. Perhaps the best known slave narrative was *The Narrative of the Life of Frederick Douglass, An American Slave*, published in 1845. At the time, Douglass had been speaking throughout the North about the evils of slavery, and he was one of the most widely admired African Americans of his day.

Another popular slave narrative in the Midwest was the autobiography of William Heyman, who was the first slave to publish his own poetry. One widely read slave narrative was *Incidents in the Life of a Slave Girl* by Harriet Jacobs. Jacobs was the mother of two small children who suffered under a brutal owner. Finally, in 1835 at age twenty-three, after years of mistreatment, she hid in a tiny crawlspace above a porch built by her grandmother and uncle, both freed slaves.

The space was nine feet by seven feet with a sloping ceiling three feet at the high end. Jacobs couldn't turn over while lying down without hitting her shoulder. Mice crawled over her, and there was no light or ventilation. Fortunately, her children had been bought by a friendly lawyer and were living in the same house. Harriet could watch while they played outside through a peephole she drilled. Incredibly, she lived in the crawlspace for seven years, coming out briefly at night.

In 1842, Harriet escaped, sailing to Philadelphia, then traveling to New York City by train. Harriet would later move to Rochester, New York, where she became involved with the abolitionist movement, working with Frederick Douglass. During the Civil War, Jacobs helped raise money for black refugees. After the war she worked to improve the conditions of the recently-freed slaves. She died in her late 80s.

Slave narratives described the brutality of slave life.

The Abolition Movement was strengthened in the 1840s by the presence of Frederick Douglass. Douglass, an escaped slave, was a powerful speaker who told horrifying stories of his experiences as a slave. Before Douglass came on the scene, few abolitionists had actually met or spoken to an African American slave. Douglass, with his brilliant speeches and powerful writing, gave Northerners their first real understanding of the injustice of slavery.

Brown met Frederick Douglass in 1847 when the former slave was touring the Northeast and Western frontier to persuade audiences of the evils of slavery. Douglass was deeply impressed by John Brown. He said, "Though a white gentleman, [Brown] is in sympathy a black man, and as deeply interested in our cause, as though his own soul had been pierced with the iron of slavery."

During their discussion, Brown told Douglass that, "slaves had a right to gain their liberty in any way they could," even if that meant violence. It was during this meeting that Brown first described his extreme idea that he would someday lead an uprising of slaves against their masters. Until that time, Douglass, who knew the power of Southern slaveholders as well as the brutal results of the Nat Turner rebellion, had been a pacifist. He hoped to persuade Americans that the United States should not permit slavery because the Declaration of Independence was based on the premise that "all men are created equal."

Frederick Douglass was
a powerful speaker
and an outspoken
abolitionist leader.

After listening to a speech by Brown, however, Douglass began to believe that violence might be necessary to achieve the goal of emancipation. He started saying at abolitionist meetings that he would be glad to see a "revolt" of the slaves. And as Congress continued to pass laws that allowed slavery to spread, Douglass lost hope that the problem of slavery would be solved peacefully.

North Elba, New York

Gerrit Smith was another well-known abolitionist and a close supporter of Frederick Douglass. Like Douglass, he had been a member of the American Anti-Slavery Society, but had broken away to form a more active abolitionist group, The Liberty Party. Smith would later run for president as a Liberty Party candidate. He used his extensive wealth to support programs dedicated to helping freed slaves.

Freed slaves were known as "freedmen" whether they were men, women, or children.

One program was a system of land grants. Smith donated 120,000 acres of his own property in the Adirondack Mountains of New York to freed slaves and their families so they could begin a new life in the North.

When Brown heard about the land grants, he traveled to New York and introduced himself to Smith. There he made a proposal to Smith. Brown was an experienced farmer, and he told the wealthy abolitionist that many of the African Americans would have difficulty farming in the cold climate and rocky land of the Adirondacks. He offered to establish a family farm

40

of his own in the area so that he could serve as an advisor to the new African American communities.

Brown's offer was not only kind, it was almost beyond the understanding of Smith and many white Northerners. For a white man in the nineteenth century—even a committed abolitionist—to live and work among African Americans on an equal basis was extremely unusual. Despite their strong beliefs that slavery was wrong, many abolitionists—like most whites of the time—viewed African Americans with prejudice and looked down on them as people. Even in the North, African Americans had few—if any—rights. Smith liked Brown's unprejudiced idea, however, and agreed to sell Brown property for just $1 an acre. Brown then moved his family to the African American settlement of North Elba, New York. This piece of property would remain his home for the rest of his life.

★

In 1855, Robert E. Lee was the superintendent of the U.S. Military Academy.

★

Brown spent little time in North Elba, however, leaving most of the farming to his youngest sons. His need for money kept him on the road, taking odd jobs from postmaster to surveyor. Wherever he went and whatever he did, Brown spoke out strongly for abolition. But it wasn't until 1855, however, when he received a letter from his sons in Kansas, that John Brown's life took a dramatic turn that would soon make him a nationally known figure—a figure both admired and hated.

41

Chapter 3

"BLEEDING KANSAS"

By the 1800s, America was expanding far beyond the Mississippi River across the plains and all the way to the Pacific Coast. For many Americans, this was the age of "Manifest Destiny," a widely held belief that because the United States was a unique democracy, it was clearly destined to occupy the continent from the Atlantic to the Pacific. It was our "right" to remove Native Americans, Mexicans, and anyone else in the way.

OPPOSITE: In the 1800s, pioneers crossed the rugged frontier in covered wagons that were filled with all their belongings.

43

During the 1840s, more than 300,000 Americans traveled across the Great Plains to the Pacific Coast along the famous Oregon and Santa Fe Trails. During the same decade the territory under U.S. control grew significantly. After a two-year war with Mexico ended in an American victory in 1848, much of the Southwest and all of California became American territory. Then, in 1848, gold was discovered in California, and the flood of people moving across the country became larger.

Naturally, as people moved across the country, many settled in places along the way, including the plains that are today Kansas and Nebraska. And although most Americans agreed that they had a right to settle on these lands, there was sharp disagreement about slavery and about government control in these areas.

Many settlers in western territories preferred strong control by the federal government. Government land grants and railways were essential to life on the plains, so was government help against Native American tribes who did not want to be moved off land they had inhabited. New communities, many thought, could not be established on the frontier without the proper government support.

The American president during these years, James Polk, was a Southern slave owner who wanted this huge area of new land to support slavery. He knew that for slavery to survive in the South, it would have to expand. If new free states

THE WAY THEY GO TO CALIFORNIA.

In 1848, the discovery of gold in California set off a "Gold Rush" that flooded the West with settlers.

entered the Union, slave states would eventually lose all power and influence in national affairs.

Again, the issue of slavery became the subject of hot debate across the country and in the halls of Congress. Neither side had any real hope of gaining complete victory. The only solution, as in 1820, was a compromise. Henry Clay of Kentucky, a force behind the Missouri Compromise as a young man, was instrumental as an elder statesman in helping the passage of the Compromise of 1850. That agreement contained several important provisions:

45

- California would be admitted to the Union as a free state.

- Both New Mexico and Utah were organized as territories. They would be admitted to the Union as either free or slave states, based on their constitutions at the time of application.

- Slave trading was prohibited in the District of Columbia, but slavery was not abolished outright.

- Severe fugitive slave laws would be enacted to protect the rights of Southern slave owners.

The Compromise of 1850, like the Missouri Compromise, did not put the issue of slavery to rest. In fact, in some ways, it made the situation worse. Northern abolitionists were deeply opposed to the Fugitive Slave Laws, which said that anyone who helped an escaped slave could be prosecuted.

Despite the growing division between North and South, newspapers in the 1850s urged people to move to the Great Plains. The land was fertile, and inexpensive. A pioneer family, papers claimed, could prosper on the frontier prairie. Thousands of Americans headed for the Kansas and Nebraska territories

The newspapers' promises, however, did not come true for many pioneers. Life was hard, and the controversies that were dividing the rest of the United States followed Americans west. As Western territories asked to join the Union, the North and South again disagreed about whether or not the new states should be "free" or "slave."

The Kansas-Nebraska Act

In 1844, a bill was introduced to Congress to establish the new Territory of Nebraska, a huge region west of Missouri that included the land that is Kansas and Nebraska today. Making the area an official territory meant that Native American land would be taken and the tribes forced to relocate. Courts and other government bodies would be set up, and the area would be under American governmental protection.

Missouri residents, naturally, had a great deal of interest in what happened in the neighboring territory. They were concerned about the issue of slavery in the new land. Many believed that if Missouri was surrounded by free states, slaves there would have easy escape routes. Thus, Missouri's existence was threatened by a free Nebraska territory, and it quickly became a political issue in Missouri.

In 1854, the Kansas-Nebraska Act attempted to address the issue. Senator David R. Atchison of Missouri sponsored the bill, which divided the Nebraska Territory into two regions. Doing so, Atchison and others believed, would permit the region's eventual entry into the Union as two separate states, one "slave" and one "free." This sentiment was expressed by a pro-slavery group in Missouri, which issued a statement that "we, the South, be permitted to peaceably possess Kansas, while the North, on the same privilege, be permitted to possess Nebraska Territory."

Newspapers in the 1850s urged people like these pioneers to move to the Great Plains, claim land, and build new lives.

The problem with this stand, however, was that both the Nebraska and Kansas portions of the Territory sat above the southern border of Missouri. More than thirty years before, the Missouri Compromise had banned slavery in new territories north of that line.

Northern lawmakers and abolitionists wanted the Missouri Compromise upheld, and slavery outlawed in the new territories. The South, however, wanted the Missouri Compromise repealed. It recognized that unless the Compromise was overturned, slave states would gradually become outnumbered because most of the new territory in the growing country was north of

Missouri's southern boundary. Eventually, the balance of power would shift and slavery would be prohibited everywhere.

Until the Compromise was overturned, it became the policy of Southern lawmakers to prevent the organization of new territories. It also became policy to insist on rights to slave ownership in any new territory, to do everything to secure those rights, and, if unsuccessful, to dissolve the Union.

If the passage of the Kansas-Nebraska Act had depended only on pressure from Southern lawmakers to overturn the Missouri Compromise, it would never have passed. As it happened, however, a Midwestern senator, Stephen Douglas of Illinois, became involved in helping the act pass. Douglas's position had nothing to do with slavery. He was acting to bring an important business to the largest city in his state.

At that time, plans were being drawn up for tracks to be laid from a midwestern city across the plains, over the Rocky Mountains all the way to the Pacific Ocean. Douglas hoped to make Chicago one end of the first transcontinental railroad. Before a company would lay tracks west from Chicago, however, it had to be assured that the lands would eventually become states under federal power.

Douglas wanted to admit all lands west of Missouri as states, so he added an important amendment to the Kansas-Nebraska Act. The amendment overruled the Missouri Compromise and replaced it with the law from the Compromise of 1850, which stated that the question of slavery would be settled by a vote of the residents of the territory rather than by the federal government. That amendment guaranteed the passage of the act.

The Kansas-Nebraska bill, signed into law on May 30, 1854, was a huge

Illinois senator Stephen Douglas played a key role in the passage of the Kansas-Nebraska Act.

success for the South. The North, on the other hand, viewed the Kansas-Nebraska Act as a betrayal. Most Northerners refused to accept it. Instead, many threw their support behind a new political party, the Republican Party, which was in favor of new rail lines, free land in the West, and strongly opposed to slavery. The Kansas-Nebraska bill also laid out the rules for setting up the first election and gave every advantage to slave-holders and supporters. The Fugitive Slave Laws of 1850 were truly in effect in the territory before the vote—anti-slavery people there who helped slaves escape could themselves be jailed and thus unable to vote. Many anti-slavery voters, such as U.S. soldiers, who made up much of Kansas' population, were specifically excluded from the vote.

The "Border Ruffians"

Even before the bill was signed into law, Northern abolitionists began urging anti-slavery settlers to go to Kansas. Similar societies in the South worked to get pro-slavery activists to Kansas. As a result, partisans for both sides poured into the territory.

★

In 1855, Andrew Johnson was the governor of Tennessee.

★

On March 30, 1855, the residents of Kansas were supposed to vote on whether Kansas would become a slave or free territory. That day, supporters of slavery from Missouri rode into Kansas more than 5,000 strong. These "Border Ruffians" were determined to achieve their aims by whatever means possible. They intimidated voters and stuffed the ballot boxes with illegal ballots. In one region with 3,000 voters, more than 6,300 ballots were cast. Even though the vote was widely viewed as unfair, when the results were tallied, Kansas had voted in favor of slavery.

The new pro-slavery legislature passed laws that placed severe penalties on anyone who even spoke out against slavery. People who helped fugitive slaves could legally be put to death or sentenced to ten years of hard labor in prison.

51

On March 30, 1855, "Border Ruffians" rode into Kansas to illegally sway the vote in favor of slavery.

The Brown Family

Among the anti-slavery settlers who had taken up the challenge to keep Kansas free was Florella Adair, Brown's father's half-sister, and her husband, Samuel. The Adairs, like all members of the extended Brown clan, were staunch abolitionists.

Five of John Brown's sons followed the Adairs to Kansas. Their journey was a fearsome one. They left Ohio in October 1854, traveling by water to Chicago, and remaining in Illinois through the winter. Once the ice broke, they resumed their journey on the Missouri River. Cholera broke out on the boat, however, and Brown's four-year old grandson, Austin, died. When the boat put into port at Waverly, Missouri, the Brown family went ashore to bury the child. The boat's captain did not wait for them to return, leaving them stranded on the banks of the river.

Left to find their way to Kansas on foot, the Brown family begged assistance at nearby farmhouses, but they were turned away. The Missourians had noted their Northern accents and figured they were abolitionists.

The Browns finally arrived in Kansas in April 1855. They settled near the Adairs in an area called Osawatomie. Shortly after the Browns' arrival in Kansas, John Brown, Jr. wrote to his father that, "Now Missouri is not alone in the undertaking to make this a slave state. Every slave-holding state from Virginia to Texas is furnishing men and money to fasten slavery upon this glorious land by means no matter how foul." He went on to say that all of the Brown sons were determined to fight. But the anti-slavery forces needed arms "more than bread." "We want you to get for us these arms," he pleaded.

Brown had no desire to go to Kansas. He was fifty-five years old and tired from years of hard work and failure. His son's letter, however, convinced him that the "Free Soilers" needed him.

The next day, Brown, accompanied by his son-in-law Henry Thompson, packed a wagon and headed west. Along the way, he collected weapons from abolitionist supporters, declaring, "I'm going to Kansas to make it a free state."

In Detroit, Brown met up with his son Oliver, who joined him on his journey. When they arrived in Waverly, Brown decided he did not like the idea of his grandson being buried "amidst the ruffian-like people" of Missouri. He removed the boy's body from its grave and brought it along with him to Kansas to be buried in free soil.

When Brown arrived in Kansas in October 1855, he was shocked by what he found. His family was suffering from starvation and illness. Brown set to work nursing his relatives back to health and improving their living conditions. Within weeks, he built two new log cabins. He put the homestead in order, preparing it to weather the upcoming winter. The new compound was now called: "Brown's Station."

The Conflict Heats Up

The Kansas vote did not mean the end of the battle over slavery. A convention of Free Soil supporters was held in Topeka later in 1855. At the convention, delegates declared the pro-slavery Kansas legislature illegal. They also drafted a constitution of their own, calling for Kansas to be admitted to the Union as a Free State.

Tensions between the two sides ran high. Articles by reporter James Redpath gave a glimpse of what life in the "Wild West" had become:

In this region when men went out to plow they always took their rifles with them, and always tilled in companies of from five to ten . . . Whenever two men approached each other, they came up pistol in hand, and the first salutation invariably was: 'Free State or Proslave?' It not infrequently happened that the next sound was the report of a pistol.

John Brown, Jr. was the captain of a small band of about 100 "Free Staters" who called themselves the Pottowatomie Rifles, taking the name from the settlement where they lived—a settlement named for the tribe that had been relocated from Ohio years before. They frequently had shouting matches with their pro-slavery neighbors, but had so far been able to avoid violence.

But as 1855 turned into 1856, the situation deteriorated. The Browns heard alarming stories of pro-slavery activity: A free state supporter was hacked to death, and his body left on his own doorstep. A force of 400 Southerners was marching into the Kansas territory.

James Redpath was a journalist and abolitionist.

President Franklin Pierce, a Southern sympathizer, announced that organizing any Free Soil resistance would be considered treason.

The Browns were afraid and angry. On May 21, they learned that hundreds of Border Ruffians had marched on the anti-slavery stronghold of Lawrence, Kansas. They had sacked the town, burning down the Free-State Hotel in the process.

Brown was enraged. "Something must be done to show these barbarians that we, too, have rights," he said. Then he gathered a small band of supporters and told them to prepare for a "secret mission."

Brown's son, afraid that Brown might do something reckless, urged his father to stay in camp. But the older man refused. Sticking a revolver into his belt, he led a party of fewer than a dozen followers off in the direction of Pottowatomie Creek, in southeastern Kansas.

The Pottowatomie Massacres

Many settlers along Pottowatomie Creek were pro-slavery members of the Law and Order Party. It was toward these homesteads that Brown and his company headed on the night of May 24, 1856, with vengeance in their hearts. Brown's goal, in his own words, was "to sweep the Pottowatomie of all Pro-Slavery men living on it."

The first stop was the home of James Doyle. Brown banged on the door and demanded that Doyle and his family step outside. When they opened the door, Brown's followers dragged Doyle and two of his sons away from the house. They then attacked the three men with swords, brutally murdering them. While Brown did not actually commit the murders—he supposedly watched as if in a trance—he did fire a single bullet into the body of James Doyle before leaving the scene. At Brown's direction, Doyle's wife, daughter, and a teenaged son were spared.

The next stop on their bloody rampage was the Wilkinson homestead, where Allen Wilkinson was kidnapped and murdered. Weapons and saddles were

This "Free-Soil" broadside was a call to arms against pro-slavery forces in Kansas.

stolen before the gang moved on to the house of James Harris. There, a pro-slavery supporter named William Sherman was murdered. More weapons, saddles, and a horse were taken.

News of the midnight killings swept through the area. Pro-slavery forces launched a manhunt. Brown hid in the woods while U.S. troops and

Missouri militiamen searched for him and his band of loyal cohorts.

Meanwhile, Brown's sons, John Jr., and Jason, who did not participate in the raid, were severely beaten. John Jr. was held prisoner for four months, and suffered a mental breakdown behind bars. Brown's Station was burned to the ground.

Reporter James Redpath, an abolitionist himself, stumbled across Brown hiding in the woods. He described the discovery in his newspaper, *Crusader of Freedom:*

> *Near the edge of a creek, a dozen horses were tied, already saddled for a ride for life, or a hunt after southern invaders . . . Old Brown himself stood near the fire. He was poorly clad, and his toes protruded from his boots . . .*

> *. . . after every meal, the old man would retire to the densest solitudes. He would say that the Lord had directed him in visions; that for himself, he did not love warfare, but peace.*

Redpath then went on to report that Brown himself was unapologetic for the death and destruction he had caused. He said that not only was his deed justified, but that it was ordered directly by God.

The Cycle of Violence

Revenge by pro-slavery forces came quickly. The governor of Kansas declared the territory in a state of war. Pro-slavery activists rampaged through

Lawrence, killing one man. Free Soilers answered the violence by attacking pro-slavery forces. Another pro-slavery gang, numbering more than 300 strong, then attacked Brown and 40 of his supporters at Osawatomie. Brown, fighting valiantly, was able to drive his attackers away, but not before the town of Osawatomie was burned. Even more tragically for Brown, his son Frederick, who was not involved in the battle, was ambushed and killed.

This period of lawlessness earned the territory the nickname of "Bleeding Kansas." A civil war, and a preview of the terrible conflict that would soon grip the nation, enveloped the territory. Between May and September of 1856, fifty-five people died in politically motivated raids and riots.

"Osawatomie Brown"

As a result of his actions, Brown became a celebrity. When he rode into Lawrence, large, cheering crowds greeted him. It was "as if the President had come to town." James Redpath's newspaper reports of the battle propelled Brown to national attention. He was praised across the North as an abolitionist hero. On Broadway, a play entitled "Osawatomie Brown" presented Brown as a hero and drew packed houses. Brown's days as a failed businessman and anonymous abolitionist were over. He was now a larger-than-life figure, with larger-than-life plans for an all-out attack on the institution of slavery.

59

Chapter 4

THE SECRET SIX

Using his newfound fame, John Brown made his way to the Northeast to raise funds. One of his first stops, in January 1857, was at the office of Franklin Sanborn, the young secretary for the Massachusetts State Kansas Committee. Sanborn, like Brown, was a strong abolitionist and was eager to keep Kansas free of slavery by any means possible.

OPPOSITE: By 1857, John Brown was a national anti-slavery figure with growing influence.

"The Weeping Time"

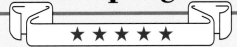

★ ★ ★ ★ ★

Throughout John Brown's fund-raising and arms gathering in 1857, the institution of slavery remained as strong as ever in the South. Ironically, though almost all Southerners supported slavery, fewer than 25 percent of all Southerners owned slaves. And of those who owned slaves, about 90 percent owned fewer than twenty slaves. Thus, the modern image of a Southern plantation worked by hundreds of slaves was not as common as many people believe.

There were, however, many plantations that were served by huge groups of slaves. One of the largest was a rice plantation located in the tidewater area of south-eastern Georgia. A wealthy man named Pierce Butler had inherited the plantation in 1837, along with the more than 450 slaves that worked and lived there. During the twenty years he owned the plantation, Butler gambled and drank away most of his large inheritance, which was worth more than $700,000 then—$10 million in today's dollars.

In Sanborn's office, Brown described his adventures on the frontier. Sanborn found Brown's stories and his personality so impressive, that he agreed on the spot to help Brown obtain money and arms

Butler ran up such huge debts that he was forced to sell all of his possessions, including, in 1857, his "moveable property," that is, his slaves. In March 1857, about 430 men, women, and children, were forced onto railway cars and steamboats and brought to a racetrack in Savannah, Georgia, where each would be sold to the highest bidder. Over two days that March, while Brown was traveling the Northeast seeking funds to fight slavery, the largest sale of human beings in the history of the United States took place at the racetrack. In a pouring rain, 436 men, women, and children were auctioned off to the highest bidders.

The sale, in which tears of those who were taken from their loved ones mixed with the raindrops, came to be known among the slaves of the South as "The Weeping Time." One witness wrote in his diary that, "It is a dreadful affair. . . . Families will not be separated, that is, husbands and wives, parents and young children. But brothers and sisters of mature age, parents and children of mature age, all other relations and the ties of home and long association will be violently severed."

The two-day sale brought $303,850. Pierce Butler, once again wealthy and free of debt, made a trip to Europe before returning to the U.S.

for his cause. For the next year, Brown was a popular figure on the abolitionist social scene. Wherever he went, excitement followed. With his rugged appearance and intense manner, he seemed like a hero from ancient days. He was praised and honored by the New England Press, and was showered with countless invitations to dinners and social events.

It was through this slow, patient process that Brown began to gather a group of financial backers willing to support his radical plans. They would become known as "The Secret Six."

First among his backers was Gerrit Smith, who already knew Brown, having sold him his farm in North Elba. Smith was considered rather nervous and eccentric. But he was also extremely wealthy and a believer in Brown. Thomas Wentworth Higginson, another backer, came from one of New England's oldest families. Higginson was a minister and an amateur boxer.

George Luther Stearns was one of the chief financiers who had supported the Emigrant Aid Company, a group that had sent Free Soilers to Kansas. Dr. Samuel Gridley Howe was a pioneer of education reforms. Theodore Parker was a controversial Unitarian Minister. Franklin Sanborn, Brown's first friend in Boston, rounded out the Secret Six.

The Plan Forms

When Brown had first left Kansas, his aim was to raise money and arms for work in Kansas. But as time passed, Brown's old idea, to incite a massive slave rebellion, began to build in his mind. He decided to form a loose chain of camps in the Blue

Ridge Mountains as bases for freedom fighters. The guerilla-style rebels would come down from their strongholds under a cover of darkness, raiding Southern plantations and arming slaves.

Attacking the federal arsenal at Harpers Ferry, Virginia, was the first and most important component of the plan. The Harpers Ferry armory held more than 100,000 weapons. Brown hoped to capture the guns and coordinate rebel activity from a nearby point. The raid would also serve as a warning to the South of what could be expected in the future.

When Brown unveiled his daring plan to the Secret Six, Sanborn was dismayed. He thought that the plan was bound to end in failure, and he strenuously argued against it. But Brown would not be swayed. Sanborn later wrote that it was,

an amazing proposition,—desperate in its character, seemingly inadequate in its provision of means, and of very uncertain results . . . But no argument could prevail against his settled purpose, with many or with few,—and

From top: Thomas Higginson, Samuel Gridley Howe, and Theodore Parker were members of the Secret Six.

65

he left us only the alternatives of betrayal, desertion, or support. We chose the last.

While the Secret Six may have had doubts at first, they soon became captivated by the plan. Frustrated by years of failed effort, they felt that action was needed. The group started raising money to pay Brown's men, to buy guns, and to commission the building of weapons that could be handed out to freed slaves once the rebellion was under way. A tentative date for John Brown's raid on Harpers Ferry was set.

The Plan Delayed

From the first, things did not go smoothly. The first hitch came when Sanborn received a blackmail threat by mail. If money wasn't paid, the letter warned, the blackmailer would expose the plot against Harpers Ferry. He also threatened to reveal the names of Brown's backers.

Smith, nervous as ever, wanted to break off the group's relationship with Brown immediately. Calling a meeting, he said, "I never was convinced of the wisdom of this scheme . . . It seems to me it would be madness to attempt to execute it." Others in the group suggested postponing the raid. Higginson was in favor of continuing as planned, calling Smith a "coward."

In the end, the Secret Six decided to delay the raid. They also made their agreement with Brown "blind." In other words, they would give funds but

66

remain ignorant of all of Brown's actions. This arrangement, they thought, would protect them from criminal liability in the event that Brown was caught.

Last but not least, Brown was sent back to Kansas, a strategic move designed to conceal his Virginia plans from prying eyes. While Brown remained safely in Kansas, the Secret Six would continue raising money until the time was right. Then Brown would return and lead the raid on Harpers Ferry.

In 1858, Abraham Lincoln lost a senatorial campaign in Illinois to Stephen Douglas.

The Missouri Raid

The diversionary tactic would only work if Brown could make his presence widely known in Kansas. Brown did this in December 1858, when he and a few followers crossed the border into Missouri. They attacked two pro-slavery strongholds and freed eleven slaves.

News of the Missouri raid made the national papers, and Brown, again, was an abolitionist hero. But the raid produced unforeseen consequences. One man was killed, and Brown found himself labeled a murderer, with a reward of $250 placed on his head.

Furthermore, in the year since Brown had been away, the violence in Kansas had died down. A fragile peace was in place. Now Brown was single-handedly threatening to stir it up. Even the abolitionists there could not support Brown if violence were to erupt again.

67

Brown also had the responsibility of the eleven fugitive slaves. His most pressing need was to help them get to safety in the North. Fugitive Slave Laws made the escapees, and anyone who helped them, subject to penalties up to and including execution. On January 20, 1859, Brown and the slaves set out into the bitterly cold prairie winter, heading North.

The journey to freedom took nearly three months. The fugitives stayed at Underground Railway stations wherever possible. Finally, on March 12, 1859, after an exhausting journey of over a thousand miles, John Brown watched his rescued slaves board a ferry to Canada, and to freedom.

The Kennedy Farm

In the spring of 1859, Brown traveled to Boston for the last time to meet with the Secret Six. Then, in July, under the assumed name of Isaac Smith, he quietly made his way to a rented house in Maryland, just across the river from Harpers Ferry, Virginia. There, at the Kennedy Farm, Brown would hole up, gather supplies, and prepare for the upcoming raid.

Gradually, supporters made their way to the isolated cabin. They included his teenage daughter, Annie, and his daughter-in-law, Martha, who kept house and helped maintain the fiction that a "normal" family was in residence.

What later came to be known as "John Brown's Army" was an untrained group of idealists made up of sixteen whites and five African Americans. This was a smaller group than Brown had envisioned; many original recruits had changed their minds in the year since the plan had been proposed.

John Brown's rented house was called the Kennedy Farm. It was there that he met with his "army" and planned for the raid on Harpers Ferry.

Several leading abolitionists simply doubted the plan. Among those who visited Brown at the farmhouse was Frederick Douglass, who refused to join the fighters. Douglass thought that the attack on Harpers Ferry would be a serious mistake. He doubted Americans would support a raid on federal property, no matter what the purpose. In a secret meeting between Brown and Douglass in August 1859, Douglass warned Brown, "You're walking into a perfect steel-trap and you will never get out alive."

Brown, however, was determined to go ahead with the raid. On October 16, 1859, John Brown and his "army" attacked the federal armory at Harpers Ferry, Virginia.

69

Brown's Raiders

★ ★ ★ ★ ★

THE AFRICAN AMERICAN RAIDERS

Dangerfield Newby was born a slave in 1815 in Virginia and had a powerful motivation for joining Browns' Army. Newby had married a woman who was still a slave in Virginia. She was in danger of being sold, and Newby wanted to either free or buy her before she was lost to him forever. **Lewis Sheridan Leary** was born in North Carolina, but later moved to Oberlin, Ohio, a center of anti-slavery sentiment. **Shields Green** was a fugitive slave from Charleston, South Carolina. He had accompanied Frederick Douglass to his August meeting with John Brown. While Brown was unable to convince Douglass to join the raid, he did persuade Green to enter his ranks. **John Anthony Copeland, Jr.**—Lewis Leary's nephew—was a free man born in Raleigh, North Carolina, in 1834. He was considered the cleverest of all the raiders. **Osborn Perry Anderson** was born free in 1830 in Pennsylvania. He lived in Canada, where he met Brown in 1858. He wrote the only surviving eyewitness account of the raid.

THE WHITE RAIDERS

John E. Cook was born in 1830 in Haddam, Connnecticut. He met John Brown in Kansas. Cook believed that a successful raid involved taking the town of Harpers Ferry. **Charles Plummer Tidd** was a captain in Brown's Army. Born in Maine in 1834, he moved to Kansas in 1856. He joined John Brown in 1857 and was one of his closest associates, taking part in the Missouri Raid. **Jeremiah**

Goldsmith Anderson was one of Brown's lieutenants. Born in Indiana in 1833, he was the grandson of slaveholders. **Albert Hazlett** was born in Pennsylvania in 1837. Hazlett met Brown in Kansas and had participated in many raids. **Edwin Coppoc** was born in 1835. He moved to Kansas in 1858, but did not participate in any of the raids or riots there. **Barclay Coppoc** was Edwin Coppoc's younger brother, and was only twenty at the time of the raid. **William Thompson** was born in New Hampshire in 1833. Thompson was closely tied to the Browns. His sister married one of John Brown's sons; his brother was married to Brown's daughter, Ruth. **Dauphin Adolphus Thompson** was William Thompson's younger brother, born in 1838. **Stewart Taylor**, born in 1836 in Uxbridge, Canada, was the only foreigner involved in the raid. A wagon maker, he met Brown during a winter journey with the fugitive slaves. **John Kagi** was born in Ohio in 1835. His father was the village blacksmith. **Aaron Dwight Stevens** ran away from his Connecticut home at sixteen and served in the Mexican War. He met Brown in 1856 and become one of his most loyal followers. **William H. Leeman** was the youngest of the raiders. He fought with Brown at Osawatomie. **Francis Jackson Merriam** was born into a staunch abolitionist family in Massachusetts in 1837. Determined to help end slavery, he sought out Brown and asked to join the company. **Owen Brown** was Brown's third son. He was one of Brown's most stalwart lieutenants, having both enormous physical strength and determination. **Watson Brown** had looked after the Brown family when his brothers left for Kansas. **Oliver Brown** was the youngest surviving Brown son. He had accompanied his father to Kansas in 1855 and to North Elba in 1856.

Chapter 5

THE RAID ON HARPERS FERRY

Brown's plan was simple—but deeply flawed. His goal was to take the town and the armory, where 100,000 weapons were stored. His "Army of Liberation" would then arm the slaves that came forward with one of the thousand pikes—long wooden poles with sharp points—he had had made in Connecticut. But Brown had no backup plan, and no plan for how to escape Harpers Ferry after the raid was completed.

OPPOSITE: The Harpers Ferry armory fire engine house, later to become known as "John Brown's Fort," served as the base of operations for the raiders.

73

Most of Brown's raiders were young men—both African Americans and whites. Three of the raiders were Brown's sons.

Brown's force was comprised of only twenty-one men, most with limited military experience. There were only five African Americans in the company. Other freedmen, afraid to risk capture and be returned to bondage, had refused to join his band. The army was not well equipped, since some of the weapons Brown had been expecting had never arrived.

Another problem was communication. Brown did not contact the slaves in the area directly to tell

John Brown

them of the planned attack. Brown just assumed that when the slaves saw the opportunity arise, they would take it and join the revolt.

Harpers Ferry was not an ideal target either. Two rivers, the Potomac and Shenandoah, converged on the eastern side of the town, leaving only one possible route for escape. The terrain was mountainous. There were few slaves in the district, and most were relatively well off house servants, with less incentive to escape or revolt than field slaves.

★

In 1856, Robert E. Lee had freed his slaves, calling slavery a "moral and political evil."

★

Furthermore, Nat Turner's earlier slave rebellion was still in the minds of Harpers Ferry residents. Frederick Douglass believed that the town would be quick to call in massive military force in the event of a second uprising. If this were to happen, John Brown's ill-prepared little troop would stand no chance.

But despite the odds against them, Brown was confident. He said that they would make a few "midnight raids upon the plantations, in order to give those who are willing among the slaves an opportunity of joining us or escaping; and it matters little whether we begin with many or few." On Sunday, October 16, 1859, John Brown's Army proceeded with their reckless plan.

On the morning of the raid, the band awoke early and read the Bible. Brown expected his army to accomplish their task without bloodshed. He told them, "And now, Gentlemen, let me impress

75

this one thing upon your minds. You all know how
dear life is to you, and how dear your life is to
your friends. And in remembering that, consider
that the lives of others are as dear to them as yours

John Brown

Brown and his men left Kennedy Farm for Harpers Ferry just after sundown on the evening of October 16, 1859.

are to you. Do not, therefore, take the life of anyone, if you can possibly avoid it; but if it is necessary to take life in order to save your own, then make sure work of it."

77

John Brown's Army left Kennedy Farm just after sundown. They crossed the Potomac River, then walked all night through heavy rain towards Harpers Ferry, Virginia. They reached the town at around 4:00 in the morning.

The Raid Begins

The raiders cut the telegraph wires leading to and from the town. Then they launched their attack. The first targets were the federal armory and arsenal. Brown's troops took them easily, as they were guarded only by a single night watchman. The armory fire engine house, later to become known as "John Brown's Fort," served as the base for their operations. It was also used as a prison for captured hostages. The "fort" was guarded at various times by Albert Hazlett, Edwin Coppoc, and Osborn Perry Anderson. Others in the Army were assigned to a supply house in the mountains, or to round up hostages and secure the bridges.

The second objective was Hall's Rifle Works, which was a supplier of weapons to the Federal government. A group of raiders, led by John Kagi, captured it easily. Then Brown sent a party of soldiers to take over a nearby plantation, owned by a descendant of George Washington. There, Colonel Lewis W. Washington was taken prisoner.

Meanwhile, Brown sought control of the main railway bridge, and made his first major mistake. As a train approached the town, the baggage master noticed the raiders. He rushed off to warn the passengers of the danger. One of Brown's men shouted, " Halt!" then fired. The baggage master, a free African American named Hayward Shepherd, was shot and killed.

Inexplicably, Brown allowed the train to continue on its way. The news reached Washington by mid-morning, and President Buchanan quickly notified the military. Forces under the leadership of Colonel Robert E. Lee were quickly sent out to combat the raiders.

Meanwhile, Brown's army was rounding up Harpers Ferry's citizens. Up to sixty people were held hostage in the firehouse. Most were guards and other workers who had been captured during the attack. Others were citizens and slave owners. Colonel Washington was also confined in the firehouse.

Now Brown made his second error. He stayed put. The clock was ticking, and Brown made no further move. As the hours passed, the raiders' chance for escape, or for success, was dwindling. Yet Brown still refused to act. In the morning, he calmly ordered breakfast for the hostages from a nearby restaurant.

Robert E. Lee was sent by President Buchanan to fight Brown's raiders.

79

Unfortunately for the raiders, Brown had overlooked another building that contained firearms. These had been removed from the armory for safekeeping during a flood and were kept in a stock house at the far end of the armory grounds. Harpers Ferry residents were able to quietly arm themselves from this hidden cache.

While Brown waited in vain for slaves to join him in the raid, the people of Harpers Ferry

After the Harpers Ferry attack, residents armed themselves, and the raiders were trapped in the "fort." When residents opened fire, many of Brown's men were shot.

surrounded the "fort." They then opened fire. The raiders were pinned down. The barrage was especially heavy at the Rifle Works. Kagi, Copeland and Leary were forced to abandon their position and run for cover.

Dangerfield Newby was the first raider to be killed in the shooting. Kagi and Leary, trying to escape the Rifle Works, were shot dead in the Shenandoah River. Copeland was captured, and a slave who had joined the revolt was drowned. In total, eight of Brown's company were killed or captured during the exchange of gunfire. Many of the town's defenders were also killed.

At mid-day, Brown tried to arrange a truce with the local citizens. He was rebuffed with gunfire. Stevens and Watson Brown were both mortally wounded by the shots. In another incident, William Thompson shot and killed the mayor, Fontaine Beckham. Witnesses were enraged by what they considered to be an unprovoked attack. In reprisal, they captured and executed Thompson on the spot. By nightfall, half of the raiders were dead or dying. The situation was deteriorating by the hour.

The military arrived at daybreak on the 17th. They quickly charged across the bridge and stormed into town, effectively cutting off any hope of escape for Brown and his men. Brown's army, or what was left of it, was surrounded.

Only a few raiders were able to escape the trap. John Cook, who had been sent with wagons back to their base in Maryland, was able to flee unobserved.

Owen Brown, Francis Jackson Meriam, Barclay Coppoc and Charles Plummer, who were manning a supply house on the heights, were able to see the armory from their position. They realized that there was no chance of helping their comrades. They decided to try and save themselves by fleeing

When the military arrived at daybreak on October 17, Brown and his men were trapped.

into the hills. Osborn Perry Anderson and Albert Hazlett also managed to escape. Brown's remaining "army" now had no choice but to hole up in the fire engine house. The fighting continued through the night.

At midmorning of the 18th, the U.S. Marines, under the command of Robert E. Lee, arrived. When the raiders looked out the window of their fortress, they were shocked to see row upon row of Marines surrounding them. Lee instructed his marines not to allow anyone to escape from the firehouse. A young lieutenant, J.E.B. Stuart—who would later serve under Lee in the Confederacy—

J.E.B. Stuart brought Brown the terms of surrender.

approached the firehouse under a white flag, and handed over a note. It said that if the raiders surrendered, their lives would be spared.

Brown refused. He demanded that the military retreat halfway across the bridge to allow the raiders to escape. At Brown's refusal to surrender, Colonel Lee gave a signal to his men to attack. Using a ladder as a battering ram, the Marines broke down the doors to the firehouse. In a vicious, bloody battle, most of the raiders were killed, including Oliver, the second of Brown's sons. In an account of the raid, a Marine named Isaac Green, who led the charge on the fire house, described the last few minutes of the doomed raid:

Three or four of my men came rushing in like tigers, as a storming assault is not a play-day sport. They bayoneted one man skulking under the engine, and pinned another fellow up against the rear wall, both being instantly killed. I ordered the men to spill no more blood. The other insurgents were at once taken under arrest, and the contest ended. The whole fight had not lasted over three minutes. My only thought was to capture, or, if necessary, kill, the insurgents, and take possession of the engine-house.

I have often been asked to describe Brown's appearance. I can only recall the fleeting picture of an old man kneeling with a carbine in his hand, with a long gray beard falling away from his face, looking quickly and keenly toward the danger that he was aware had come upon him. He was not a large man, being perhaps five feet ten inches when he straightened up in full. None of the prisoners were hurt. They were badly frightened and somewhat starved . . . . Brown had, at the time, only five or six fighting men, and I think he himself was the only one who showed fight after I entered the engine-house.

It had been less than thirty-six hours since the raid was begun. Brown's ill-fated attempt to start a slave rebellion was over.

85

Was He Sane?

Since the time of the raid, people have debated John Brown's state of mind. Judging by his action in Harpers Ferry, it is easy to see why many think he might have been insane. Brown's plan was so poorly conceived there was really no chance of his getting out of Harpers Ferry alive.

An insanity defense was even suggested for his trial. His lawyer wanted to present evidence that insanity ran in Brown's family. But Brown refused to plead insanity, saying he was as sane as any man. His judge, jailers, and reporters writing on his trial all agreed. Governor Wise of Virginia, who spent three hours with him immediately after the raid, said, "They are themselves mistaken who take him to be a madman." Neither did his fellow abolitionists find him unstable.

The question that many people have asked over the years is: Why did John Brown launch a raid that was doomed?

One possibility is that Brown wanted to die. He had suffered a miserable, hard life, and he was tired. Perhaps this final act was not an act of madness, but one of suicide.

Another possibility was that Brown really believed the raid was his God-ordained destiny. There is no question that Brown was religious to the point of fanaticism, and he had said many times he was following God's will when questioned about his violent actions.

It may also be possible that his own death did not come into Brown's equation. Brown wanted to end slavery. He assessed the situation and discovered that, whether or not he succeeded, the raid would achieve his goal: to speed the end of slavery. In this view he was correct. Even though the raid "failed," the war against slavery was eventually won.

Exaggerated depictions of the capture filled the newspapers after the raid. Brown, shown here waving a rifle, was actually old and bearded when he was captured.

Capture and Trial

Immediately after the fight, Brown was carried out of the engine house by a number of militia men. He had fallen unconscious, but he came to while lying on the ground outside the "fort." A detail of Marines was assigned to carry him to the paymaster's office, where he was imprisoned until further orders were received.

Upon hearing the news of Brown's capture, Governor Wise of Virginia traveled to Harpers Ferry immediately. He wanted to see Brown for himself. Wise was surprised by what he found. Brown was composed and articulate. The Governor interrogated him for three hours. "He is cool, collected and indomitable," Wise said, "and he inspired me with great trust in his integrity as a man of truth."

The next day, Brown and four of his companions —Copeland, Edwin Coppoc, Green, and Stevens— were escorted by the Marines to Charlestown, Virginia, where they were turned over to the civil authorities. Brown was not placed in handcuffs and was allowed to walk on his own.

The country's reaction to the raid was swift and intense. In the South, newspaper accounts greatly exaggerated the force of the Brown's army, claiming that there had been 800 armed raiders. This notion terrified the slave owners. They were horrified by the idea of Northerners arming slaves, and of free blacks forming militias that could come into the South and fight on the slaves' behalf. The South feared that the government would not be able to protect them against future raids, and resolved to take the matter into their own hands.

Northerners were also shocked by the violence. Abolitionists sought to distance themselves from the plot, afraid of the backlash that might result.

89

Newspapers hinted that Frederick Douglass was involved. Even though Douglass had refused to support Brown's plan, he feared for his life and fled the country to Canada.

Old Friends Fall

For the Secret Six, Brown's capture was a disaster. They waited fearfully, wondering if Brown would give them away. Smith suffered a nervous breakdown and was taken to an insane asylum. Howe, Stearns and Sanborn fled to Canada. Both Howe and Stearns remained there, but Sanborn returned home to Concord, Massachusetts, where federal marshals tried to capture him, but the townspeople turned out to protect him.

This version of Brown's capture shows him as a helpless old man, clutching a young member of his army.

Reverend Parker was dying of tuberculosis. Upon hearing of Brown's fate, he called Brown a "saint." Higginson did not try to evade capture. He even went so far as to consider a last minute attempt to save Brown.

Brown's trial and sentencing took place at the court house in Charlestown, Virginia.

Higginson claimed that he felt responsible for John Brown. "I should have realized the need to protect him from himself," he said.

Brown was brought to trial in the Virginia Court in Charlestown on November 2, 1859. It was obvious that he would be convicted of murder. But the trial was dramatic. As it concluded, Brown asked to be allowed to speak. He then went on to make an oft-quoted address to the Court that defined his position since that time.

I have, may it please the court, a few words to say. In the first place, I deny everything but what I have all along admitted—the design on my part to free slaves. I intended certainly to have made a clean thing of that matter, as I did last winter, when I went into Missouri and took slaves without the snapping of a gun on either side, moved them

John Brown was hanged in Virginia on December 2, 1859. The execution was highly publicized, but closed to the public.

through the country, and finally left them in Canada. I designed to do the same thing again, on a larger scale. That was all I intended. I never did intend murder, or treason, or the destruction of property, or to excite or incite slaves to rebellion, or to make insurrection . . . .

John Brown

The court acknowledges, as I suppose, the validity of the law of God. I see a book kissed here which I suppose to be the Bible, or at least the New Testament. That teaches me that all things whatsoever I would that men should do to me, I should do even so to them. I feel no consciousness of my guilt. I have stated from the first what was my intention, and what was not. I never had any design against the life of any person, nor any disposition to commit treason, or excite slaves to rebel, or make any general insurrection. I never encouraged any man to do so, but always discouraged any idea of any kind.

Three days after the trial began, John Brown, along with John Copeland Jr., Edwin Coppoc, John Cook, who had been captured in Maryland, and Shields Green, were sentenced to death.

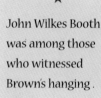

★

John Wilkes Booth was among those who witnessed Brown's hanging.

★

Governor Wise received stacks of hate mail and death threats from supporters of Brown. Responding to rumors and threats that Brown would be helped to escape, he called out the state militia and cadets from the Virginia Military Institute and set an armed guard around Brown's cell.

On the day of the hanging, residents of Harpers Ferry were warned to stay in their houses and to prepare to defend themselves if necessary. The execution site was closed to the public. Brown was executed on the gallows on December 2, 1859. His body was taken to North Elba, New York, where it was buried.

93

Chapter 6

AFTERMATH

In the months after the trail and execution, Northerners came to view Brown as a hero. Journalist James Redpath requested a chip from the gallows from the hangman. Redpath labeled it, "A Bit of the True Cross, a Chip from the Scaffold of John Brown," and kept it as a relic for the rest of his life.

Frederick Douglass, writing about Brown in later years, put it this way:

> *John Brown began the war that ended American slavery and made this a free Republic. His zeal in the cause of my race was far greater than mine. I could live for the slave, but he could die for him.*

OPPOSITE: This painting, which portrays Brown as a saintly man, is an example of how the abolitionist was idealized after his death.

95

The Co-Conspirators

Most of the five surviving raiders went on to continue the fight against slavery. Charles Plummer enlisted as a private in the Twenty-First Massachusetts Volunteer Regiment of the Union Army. En route to the battle of Roanoke, Plummer came down with a fever while aboard the transport ship and died on February 8, 1862.

Barclay Coppoc fled to Iowa, and was followed there by Virginia agents who tried unsuccessfully to arrest him. He continued on to Kansas, where he risked his life several times in helping to free some Missouri slaves. He then joined the Third Kansas Infantry of the Union Army as a first lieutenant. He was killed when a train fell from a railway trestle that had had its supports burned away by the Confederate army. Osborn Perry Anderson was able to escape to Canada. He returned to the United States in 1864 and enlisted in the Union Army. He helped recruit slaves for the United States Colored Troops in Indiana and Arkansas. After the Civil War, he continued to be active in the fight for black rights. He died of tuberculosis in 1872 at the age of forty-two.

Francis Jackson Meriam escaped to Canada. Afterwards, he settled in Illinois and then enlisted in the Union Army. He served as captain in the Third South Carolina Colored Infantry. Early in the war, he married. While serving under General Grant, he was severely wounded. Meriam died in November 1865.

Owen Brown had acted as the leader of the small band of raiders that managed to escape. It was due to his physical strength and perseverance that they were all able to reach safety. Brown was the only one of the surviving raiders who did not enlist in the Union Army. He grew grapes with two of his brothers for a brief period, then moved to California. He never married, and lived a simple life on a mountain retreat that he called "Brown's Peak." He died in 1891.

"John Brown's Body"

The story of John Brown quickly became an inspirational legend. No longer was he John Brown, a crusty old abolitionist, but rather JOHN BROWN: saint, hero, and martyr to the abolitionist cause.

The legend soon spawned a popular song called "John Brown's Body." It was widely sung as a stirring anthem for the Union troops. The lyrics of one early version ran as follows:

John Brown's body lies a-mouldering in the grave,
While weep the sons of bondage whom he ventured all
  to save;
But though he lost his life in struggling for the slave,
His truth is marching on.

CHORUS:
Glory, Glory, Hallelujah!
His truth is marching on!

Union troops adopted the lyrics and melody of "John Brown's Body" as an inspirational song early in the Civil War. The chorus and melody later became Julia Ward Howe's "Battle Hymn of the Republic."

> John Brown was a hero, undaunted, true and brave;
> Kansas knew his valor when he fought her rights to
>   save;
> And now though the grass grows green above his grave,
> His truth is marching on.
> CHORUS
> He captured Harpers Ferry with his nineteen men so
>   few,
> And he frightened "Old Virginny" till she trembled
>   through and through,
> They hung him for a traitor, themselves a traitor crew,
> But his truth is marching on.
> CHORUS

Julia Ward Howe used the melody of that song, and its chorus a few years later when she composed the lyrics to *The Battle Hymn of the Republic*, one of the most famous songs to come out of the Civil War.

John Brown

The Cause of Civil Rights Went On

In April 1865, the Civil War came to a bloody close with the North victorious. In December 1865, Congress ratified the Thirteenth Amendment to the U.S. Constitution ending slavery in the United States.

But freedom was not complete. Legislatures of the Southern states passed oppressive laws designed to keep African-Americans down. These discriminatory laws were called Black Codes. Black Codes stated that any ex-slave who did not have a steady job could be arrested. He could be ordered to pay stiff fines. Prisoners who could not pay the fines were forced to work them off. African-American children could be forced to serve as unpaid apprentices in local industries. The Codes also prevented African-Americans from buying land, and denied them fair wages for their labor.

There was more work to be done to achieve true freedom for the ex-slaves. As Frederick Douglass explained, "Slavery is not abolished until the black man has the ballot."

Two additional amendments to the Constitution were still needed. The Fourteenth Amendment, which was ratified in 1868, awarded African-Americans full rights of citizenship. Although the amendment explicitly stated that no one could deny any person his full rights as a citizen, it did not explicitly mention the right to vote.

99

This engraving celebrates the passage of the Fifthteenth Amendment in 1870, which gave every man the right to vote, regardless of color. John Brown is shown in the top right, on the left. President Lincoln is top center, and Frederick Douglass is shown in the bottom left corner.

This oversight was corrected with the Fifteenth Amendment, which was passed in 1870. It gave all male citizens, regardless of color, the right to vote.

Eleven years after his failed raid on Harpers Ferry, Brown's goal was finally achieved. Slavery was no more, and the rights of African Americans as equals under the law took their rightful place in the United States Constitution.

John Brown—the tanner, farmer, failed businessman, and fiery idealist—had, in his own way, helped to open the first door of equality for all African Americans.

Glossary

abolitionism A political movement in the 1800s that sought to ban slavery. Abolitionists worked for abolition.

amendment A change to a written document such as the U.S. Constitution

assassinate To murder by sudden or secret attack

canal An artificial waterway constructed for transportation

compromise A settlement reached by mutual agreement of two opposing sides on an issue

debate A discussion of opposing opinions regarding an issue

emancipation Freedom

fugitive One who runs away

plantation A large farm in the South worked by slaves in the years before the Civil War

prejudice A negative opinion toward individuals or people of a different race, religion, social class, or other group

Reconstruction The reorganization and reestablishment of the seceded states in the Union after the American Civil War

secession Formal withdrawal from an organization

speculation Taking a financial risk in hopes of gaining large rewards

tanner A person who tans—darkens and softens—the hides of animals for clothing, footwear, covering, and other uses

territory A region of land that is not a state, but that has its own government

For More Information

Books

Barret, Tracy. *Harpers Ferry: The Story of John Brown's Raid.* (Spotlight on American History). Brookfield, CT: Millbrook Press 1993.

Collins, James. *John Brown and the Fight Against Slavery* (Gateway Civil Rights Series). Brookfield, CT: Millbrook Press, 1991.

Everett, Gwen. *John Brown: One Man Against Slavery* (Children's Library). New York: Rizzoli International, 1993.

Potter, Robert R. *John Brown: Militant Abolitionist* (American Troublemakers). Austin, TX: Raintree/Steck-Vaughn, 1994.

Scott, John & Scott. *Robert John Brown of Harpers Ferry* (Makers of American). New York: Facts on File, 1988.

Web Sites

The American Experience: John Brown's Holy War
http://www.pbs.org/wgbh/amex/brown/
A PBS site with timelines, maps, and images surrounding the life of Brown.

John Brown and the Valley of the Shadow
http://jefferson.village.virginia.edu/jbrown/master.html
A site sponsored by the University of Virginia that offers primary source material on the Harpers Ferry raid as well as photos of the Brown family and some of his "army."

Welcome to the Kennedy Farmhouse
http://www.johnbrown.org/
This Web site about Brown is centered on the restored farmhouse that was his staging area for the raid on Harpers Ferry and contains text, timelines, maps, and photos.

Index

Abolitionism, 34–35, 38

Black Codes, 99
Bleeding Kansas, 43, 54–59
Border Ruffians, 51
Brown family
  Adair, Austin (grandson), 53, 54
  Adair, Flora, 52
  Brown, Annie, 68
  Brown, Jason, 25, 58
  Brown, John, Jr., 25, 55, 58
  Brown, Frederick, 25, 59
  Brown, Martha, 68
  Brown, Oliver, 54, 71, 85
  Brown, Owen, 25, 71, 82, 97
  Brown, Ruth, 25
  Brown, Watson, 71, 81
  Day, Mary (second wife), 25
  Lusk, Dianthe (first wife), 18, 22, 23
Brown, John
  "army" of, 68, 69, 70–71, 74, 96
  attack of on Harpers Ferry, 75–85
  attitude toward slavery, 14, 16, 17, 35, 38, 41
  capture and trial, 88–93
  childhood, 11–17
  early adulthood, 18–25
  execution, 8–9, 93

financial trouble, 25, 32, 33
Harpers Ferry plan, 64–65, 69, 73
in Kansas, 54–59
Missouri raid, 67–68
religious beliefs, 14, 33, 35, 58
sanity, 86–87

Canals, 30, 31
Compromise of 1850, 45–46

Douglas, Stephen, 49–50
Douglass, Frederick, 18, 38, 39, 40, 54, 95, 99

Fifteenth Amendment, 100
Fourteenth Amendment, 99

Garrison, William Lloyd, 34–35
Grant, Ulysses, 38, 85

Harpers Ferry, 8, 65, 69, 75

Jackson, Andrew, 27, 28, 29
Jackson, Stonewall, 9, 16, 30

Kansas-Nebraska Act, 47–51

Land speculation, 28
Lee, Robert E., 22, 41, 75, 79, 84
Lincoln, Abraham, 16, 33

Manifest Destiny, 43, 44
Missouri Compromise, 18,
  20–22

Native Americans, 27, 28, 29,
  55
North Elba, New York, 40, 41,
  93

Prosser, Gabriel, 13, 14

Redpath, James, 54, 58, 95

Secret Six, 61, 64–67, 88–89
Slave narratives, 36–37
Slavery, 12–14, 29
Smith, Gerrit, 40, 41, 66

Tannery, 18, 19, 22, 23
Thirteenth Amendment, 99
Turner, Nat, 23

Weeping Time, 62–63
Westward expansion, 43, 44, 46
Van Buren, Martin, 32, 33

John Brown